THE STORY OF THE
PORTLAND
TRAIL BLAZERS

CREATIVE EDUCATION

Published by Creative Education
123 South Broad Street
Mankato, Minnesota 56001
Creative Education is an imprint of The Creative Company.

DESIGN AND PRODUCTION BY **EVANSDAY DESIGN**

PHOTOGRAPHS BY AP World Wide / AP, Getty Images (Victor
Baldizon / NBAE, Andrew D. Bernstein, Vince Bucci / AFP,
Jim Cummins, Brian Drake / Time & Life Pictures, Stephen
Dunn, Allen Finstein / NBAE, Focus on Sport, Sam Frencich,
Nancy Hogue / NBAE, Joe Murphy / NBAE, Mike Powell
/ Allsport, Philip Schermeister / National Geographic,
Rocky Widner / NBAE)

LIBRARY OF CONGRESS CATALOGING-IN-PUBLICATION DATA

Frisch, Aaron.
The story of the Portland Trail Blazers / by Aaron Frisch.
p. cm. — (The NBA—a history of hoops)
Includes index.
ISBN-13: 978-1-58341-422-4
1. Portland Trail Blazers (Basketball team)—History—
Juvenile literature. I. Title. II. Series.

GV885.52P67F75 2006
796.323'64'0979549—dc22   2005051768

First edition

9 8 7 6 5 4 3 2 1

COVER PHOTO: *Sebastian Telfair*

THE STORY OF THE
PORTLAND
TRAIL BLAZERS

AARON FRISCH

CREATIVE ☕ EDUCATION

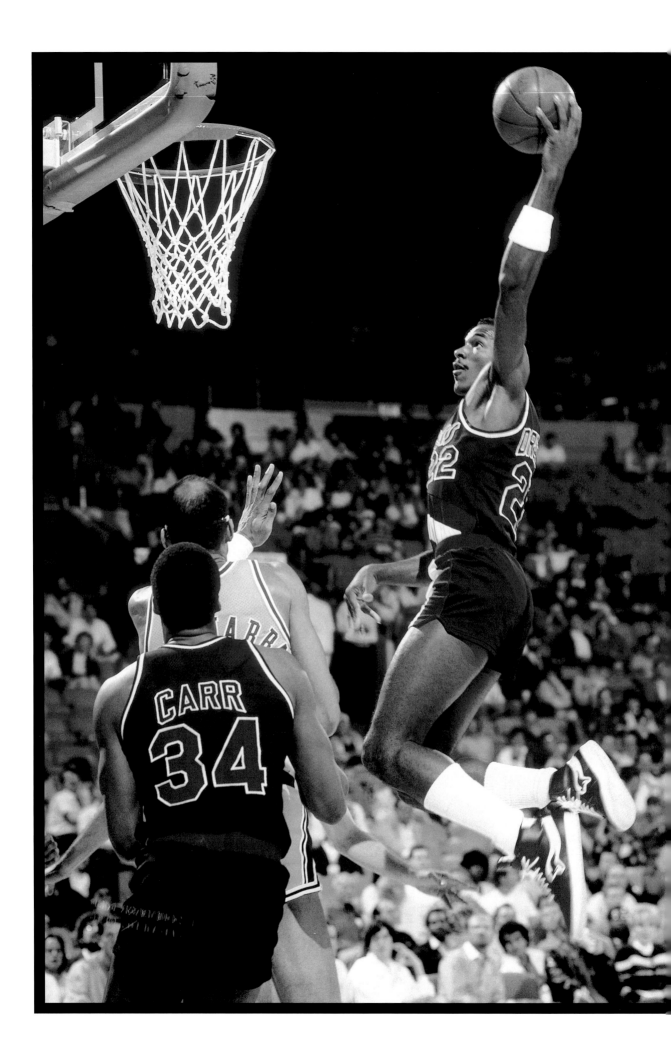

Fans called Portland

"RIP CITY," AND IT WAS A RIP-ROARING BASKETBALL TOWN. IT WAS THE EARLY 1990S, AND CLYDE "THE GLIDE" DREXLER WAS SOARING IN FOR RIM-RATTLING, CROWD-PLEASING DUNKS. JEROME KERSEY AND KEVIN DUCKWORTH WERE ELBOWING OPPONENTS ASIDE FOR REBOUNDS UNDER THE BASKET, CLIFF ROBINSON WAS SWATTING ENEMY SHOTS OUT OF THE AIR, AND TERRY PORTER WAS ZIPPING PASSES TO TEAMMATES WITH PINPOINT PRECISION. THIS CREW IN BLACK AND RED TOOK FANS ON A ROLLER-COASTER RIDE THAT INCLUDED TWO NBA FINALS APPEARANCES, ETCHING MEMORIES THAT LINGER AND CHEERS THAT ECHO STILL.

THE TRAIL BEGINS

NEARLY 200 YEARS AGO, EXPLORERS MERIWETHER Lewis and William Clark blazed a trail across the untamed American West. Their epic journey, which ended in the Pacific Northwest, opened the way for pioneers. In 1845, some of these pioneers set up a trading post that later became the city of Portland, Oregon. In 1970, the National Basketball Association (NBA) decided to place a team in this growing city. In honor of the brave explorers who put Portland on the map, the team was named the Portland Trail Blazers.

Versatile forward Sidney Wicks led the first-year Blazers with 24 points, 11 rebounds, and 4 assists a game

10

Although star center Bill Walton excelled in many areas, he was probably most dominant as a rebounder

Like most teams just starting out, the Trail Blazers lost a lot of games their first few seasons. Even though Blazers fans saw few victories in Portland's Memorial Coliseum, they were able to watch two special players—sharp-shooting guard Geoff Petrie and versatile forward Sidney Wicks. Petrie was selected with the team's first pick in the 1970 NBA Draft and quickly earned a reputation as a top outside marksman. Wicks, meanwhile, was big enough to play center and quick enough to play small forward, earning him the nickname "Mr. Everything."

As good as they were, Petrie and Wicks couldn't lead the Trail Blazers to a winning record. But in the 1974 NBA Draft, Portland drafted a 6-foot-11, redheaded center named Bill Walton. Walton could score seemingly at will, yet he was also a great passer. Portland fans were disappointed when he didn't make the Blazers into winners in his first two seasons. The big center always seemed to have foot and ankle injuries, and "Blazermaniacs" wondered when things would change.

MR. 51 For a player to score 50 points in a single game is a rare feat—one that has been achieved only twice in Trail Blazers history. When the Blazers used their first-ever draft pick in 1970 to make Princeton University guard Geoff Petrie the "Original Blazer," they knew they were getting a player who could put the ball in the basket. This was vividly demonstrated in a January 1973 game against the Houston Rockets, when Petrie—renowned for his quick release and pinpoint accuracy—poured in a career-high 51 points. When the Blazers met the Rockets again two months later, Petrie's long-range bombs torched the nets (and the Rockets) for another 51. His totals would have been even higher had the three-point line then existed in the NBA. After his playing days, Petrie spent five years as the Trail Blazers' vice president of basketball operations.

BLAZING TO THE TOP

PORTLAND HIRED A NEW COACH NAMED JACK RAMSAY in 1976. Coach Ramsay demanded that Walton and other top players such as guards Lionel Hollins and Dave Twardzik and forward Maurice Lucas play aggressive defense and unselfish offense. No player did both better than Walton, who was finally healthy and able to play his best. "For two years, I wasn't able to run up and down the court freely without…thinking about [my injuries]," Walton explained. "That's no way to play basketball."

Behind their big center, the Trail Blazers made the playoffs for the first time after the 1976–77 season, then beat the Chicago Bulls, Denver Nuggets, and Los Angeles Lakers to reach the NBA Finals. In the Finals, the Trail Blazers faced the Philadelphia 76ers and their star

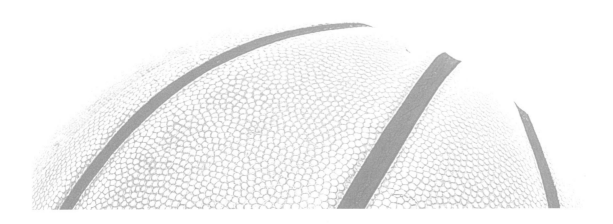

13

SUPERVISING COACH

An NBA coach for 20 years, Jack Ramsay is today enshrined in the Basketball Hall of Fame

NBA BALL

Guard Dave Twardzik posted the league's best shooting percentage in both 1976-77 and 1977-78

guard, "Dr. J" (Julius Erving). Philadelphia won the first two games. But something happened late in Game 2 that would turn the series' momentum around. Maurice Lucas and 76ers center Darryl Dawkins got into a short but spectacular fight. Dawkins was a powerful player, but "Big Mo" proved that he was not intimidated.

Inspired by Lucas's tenacity, the Blazers rebounded to win the next three games. In Game 6 in Portland, with only seconds left and the Blazers ahead 109–107, Philadelphia forward George McGinnis drove to the basket and lofted the ball up. The ball hit iron, then Walton swatted it back to midcourt as the horn sounded and fans rushed the court to celebrate. The next day, 50,000 people lined the streets of downtown Portland for a victory parade. "I'll never be able to think of that Monday without smiling," Blazers president Harry Glickman later said. "It was just such a great day for Portland and the whole state.... Everybody had signs that said, 'Rip City' or 'Red-Hot and Rollin'.'"

Portland fans prepared for another championship parade when the Blazers started 50–10 the next season. But Walton broke his foot in the first round of the playoffs, and the Blazers lost. A few months later, Walton—who felt that the Portland medical staff had not treated his injury properly—stunned Portland by announcing that he wanted to be traded, a demand that the Blazers soon met, sending him to the San Diego Clippers. Players such as center Mychal Thompson and guard Jim Paxson kept the Blazers competitive after Walton left, but they were no longer a championship contender.

Since 1976, the Trail Blazers have enjoyed 24 winning seasons and suffered only 5 losing ones

THE TITLE FIGHT

During the 1977 NBA Finals, basketball briefly turned into boxing. The star-laden Philadelphia 76ers beat the underdog Trail Blazers in Game 1 and were winning big late in Game 2 when 76ers center Darryl Dawkins threw Portland guard Bobby Gross roughly to the floor. Slim but tough Blazers forward Maurice Lucas sprinted the length of the court to challenge Dawkins. Chaos erupted as the two exchanged a flurry of punches, and players, fans, and security guards spilled onto the Philadelphia court. The two combatants were kicked out of the game, but Lucas's courage in taking on the much-larger Dawkins swung the series' momentum in Portland's favor. Good sportsmanship also prevailed. "We went back into Portland," Lucas later recalled, "and before the start of Game 3, Dawkins and I shook hands."

"RIP CITY" ROARS

IN 1984, THE BLAZERS TRADED SEVERAL PLAYERS to the Denver Nuggets for forward Kiki Vandeweghe. Not the fastest or most athletic player on the court, Vandeweghe instead used his intelligence to become a feared scorer. "He [the defender] is always going to make a mistake—leaning the wrong way, too close, the wrong foot forward, shifting his eyes," he once explained. "You just have to wait for his mistake and capitalize on it."

19

Standout forward Kiki Vandeweghe was the son of early New York Knicks great Ernie "Doc" Vandeweghe

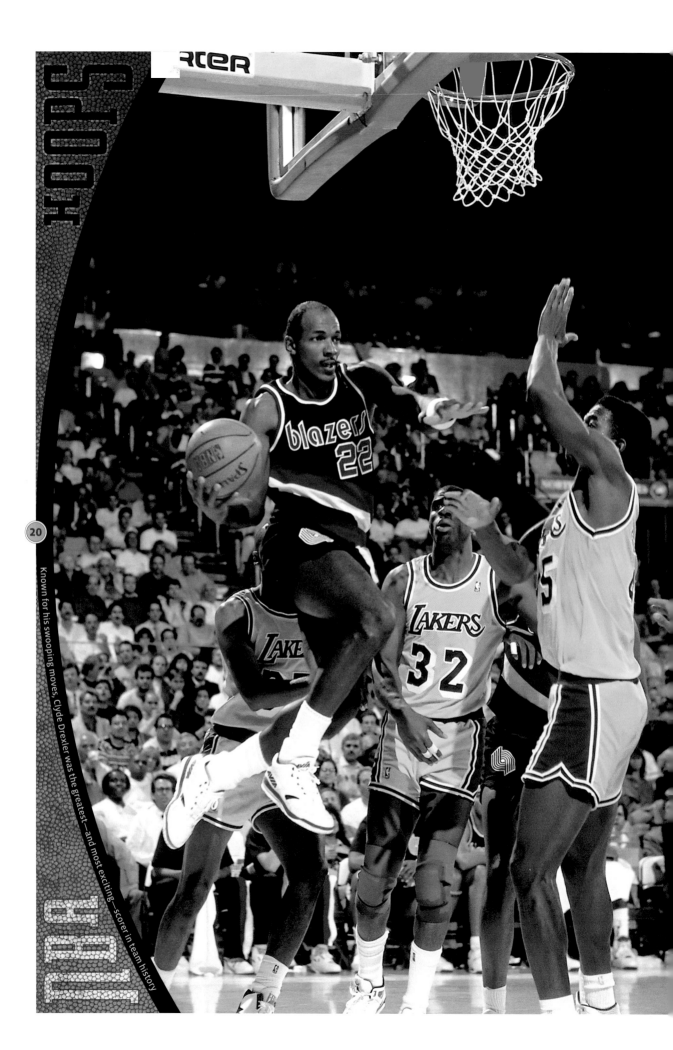

20

Known for his swooping moves, Clyde Drexler was the greatest—and most exciting—scorer in team history

The Blazers were the NBA's highest-scoring team in 1986–87. Some of the credit went to Vandeweghe, but a lot of it went to young shooting guard Clyde Drexler. Portland had selected Drexler out of the University of Houston in the 1983 NBA Draft. At first, many people thought he was just an average player who could jump. But Drexler, known as "Clyde the Glide" because of his smooth moves and great vertical leap, soon showed he could do it all.

Drexler scored plenty of points throughout the late 1980s, but the Blazers lost in the playoffs every year. In 1989, Portland promoted assistant Rick Adelman to head coach. The new coach knew his team had talent. Forward Jerome Kersey and center Kevin Duckworth formed a burly inside combination, while point guard Terry Porter paired with Drexler for a great outside attack. By trading for hardworking power forward Buck Williams, the Blazers looked like a contender again.

After the 1989–90 season, the Blazers fought their way to the NBA Finals but lost the championship to the Detroit Pistons. The next year, they

A MISSED OPPORTUNITY

In the 1984 NBA Draft, center Hakeem Olajuwon was selected first overall by the Houston Rockets, and the Trail Blazers, wanting to add size to their lineup, used the second pick to take 7-foot-1 center Sam Bowie. The Chicago Bulls then "settled" for a 6-foot-6 guard named Michael Jordan with the third pick. "We wish he [Jordan] were seven feet, but he's not," Bulls general manager Rod Thorn lamented after the draft. "There just wasn't a center available. What can you do?" But Portland fans would lament after that. Bowie would play just four mediocre, injury-plagued seasons for the Blazers. Jordan, meanwhile, would go on to lead Chicago to 6 NBA titles, win 10 league scoring titles, and cement a legacy as arguably the greatest basketball player of all time.

started the season 19–1 and finished with a 63–19 record, but lost to the Lakers in the Western Conference Finals. The loss made Drexler and his teammates more determined than ever to finally get over the hump and win another NBA title for Portland. "We're a better team than we showed," Drexler said. "We'll be back."

Drexler shot and dunked his way to an average of 25 points per game the next year and helped Portland roll through three playoff opponents. The Blazers then faced one of the toughest teams of all time in the NBA Finals: the Chicago Bulls. Drexler battled Bulls superstar Michael Jordan fiercely in the series, but the Bulls triumphed in six games.

That was the last hurrah for the Blazers. A number of the team's top players were soon traded away, and Portland slipped in the standings. Many fans were saddened in 1995 when Clyde the Glide was traded to the Houston Rockets, who promptly won the NBA championship. It seemed the exciting days in Rip City were over.

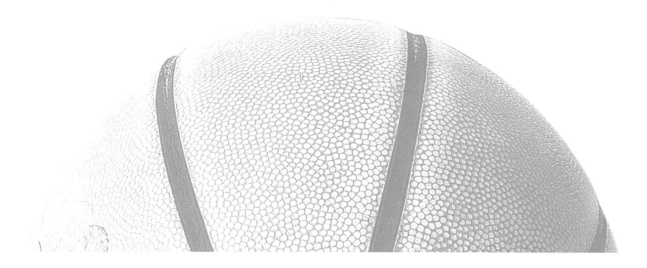

23

Jerome Kersey ranks second in Portland's record books for games played (831) and career rebounds (5,078)

STOKING ANOTHER BLAZE

AFTER DREXLER'S DEPARTURE, THE BLAZERS REBUILT around center Arvydas Sabonis. A 7-foot-3 giant from Lithuania who had played for many years in Europe, Sabonis was a skilled rebounder and shooter. He could also flip the ball behind his back or fire full-court passes with the skill of a point guard. "Arvydas and Bill Walton are the two best passing big men ever," said Milwaukee Bucks coach Mike Dunleavy. "No one else is even close."

25

A clever scorer and passer, Arvydas Sabonis was 30 years old when he played his first NBA season

The veteran leadership of Scottie Pippen helped take the Blazers to the brink of the 2000 NBA Finals

Paul Allen, the Trail Blazers' wealthy owner, paid top dollar to surround Sabonis with talent. In the late '90s, Portland fans saw some exciting performances by such players as guard Isaiah Rider and forward Rasheed Wallace. These players gave the Blazers the firepower to beat the NBA's best teams on any given night. But they were also prone to losing skids, and Rider, Wallace, and other players often threw temper tantrums and behaved badly off the court.

In 1998–99, the Blazers seemed about ready to make another run at an NBA title. With new point guard Damon Stoudamire running a fast-paced offense—and cheered on by 20,000 fans a night in the new Rose Garden in downtown Portland—the Blazers streaked all the way to the Western Conference Finals before losing to the San Antonio Spurs. A few weeks after the loss, Portland traded for All-Star guard Scottie Pippen, who had helped the Chicago Bulls win six NBA championships.

With Pippen on board, the Blazers battled their way back to the Western Conference Finals in 2000 and a showdown with the Los Angeles Lakers. The Lakers and star center Shaquille O'Neal jumped out to a three-games-to-one series lead, but the Blazers won the next two. In the deciding Game

BLAZIN' A STREAK Portland has enjoyed its share of NBA highlights since joining the league in 1970, capturing one world championship, making three NBA Finals appearances, and reaching the Western Conference Finals six times. But perhaps most remarkable of all is the Trail Blazers' consistency year after year as a formidable team. From 1976–77 to 2002–03, the Blazers made the playoffs every season but one—a staggering run of 23 playoff trips in 24 years, including 20 in a row. When the streak finally ended in 2003, the Blazers proved to be as optimistic as they are steady. "I know there's a lot of disappointed people because we didn't make the playoffs," said coach Maurice Cheeks. "But my message to them is we have something special to build on."

7, the Blazers had the Lakers on the ropes, building a 15-point lead in the fourth quarter. But Portland fans watched in pain and disbelief as the Lakers stormed back for the win. "It's tough to swallow right now," Pippen said sadly after the game, "and I'm sure it will be all summer."

The stunning collapse seemed to end the momentum that had been building in Portland, and the team made quick playoff exits the next few seasons. By 2004, the Blazers were a team with a new look. Gone were Pippen and Wallace, replaced by younger players such as forwards Zach Randolph and Shareef Abdur-Rahim. A 27–55 record (the team's worst in 32 years) in 2004–05 made it clear that Portland needed to rebuild again. But fans were confident that coach Nate McMillan and the next genera-tion of Blazers—featuring such up-and-coming youngsters as point guard Sebastian Telfair—would soon help the club blaze a trail back to glory.

It has been almost three decades since the Trail Blazers hoisted their NBA championship trophy, and more than a decade since their great seasons of the early '90s. But the Blazers have never been far from contention, and as their loyal fans have learned over more than 35 years of basketball, the wait will be well worth it when Rip City rises again.

BASKETBALL'S RICHEST OWNER

Since 1988, the Trail Blazers have been owned by one of the richest men in the world: Paul Allen. With an estimated net worth of $30 billion, Allen's fortunes stem from 1975, when, along with Bill Gates (the richest person in the world), he co-founded the Microsoft Corporation. Since his start in computer technology, he has invested in a number of other entertainment and technology companies. He has also earned a reputation as a sports owner (he also owns the Seattle Seahawks pro football team) willing to spend as much money as necessary to put a winner on the court or field. As the Trail Blazers' owner, Allen has made a pledge to Portland fans that consists of 25 points, one of which is "To continue to deliver world-class sports and entertainment experiences."

29

Despite his small size (6 feet and 160 pounds), Sebastian Telfair figured to be a big part of Portland's future

31

Burly forward Zach Randolph was among the top rebounders—and most physical players—in the NBA

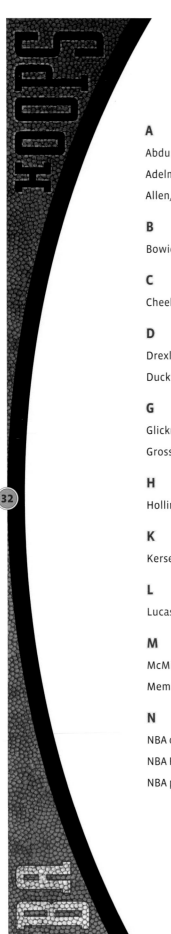